D0777615

180 Days
of Character

by Donna B. Forrest, Ed.S.

YouthLight, Inc.
P.O. Box 115 • Chapin, SC 29036
(800) 209-9774 • (803) 345-1070
Fax (803) 345-0888 • Email YLDR1@aol.com

© 1998 by
YouthLight, Inc.
Chapin, SC 29036

All rights reserved.

Design and layout by Elizabeth Madden
Project Editor Susan Bowman & Melissa White

ISBN 1-889636-10-X
Library of Congress Catalog Number

10 9 8 7 6 5 4 3 2 1
Printed in the United States of America

Dedication

To Derek and April – through the joys, laughter, tears and triumphs – the good character traits unique to each of you has inspired me beyond words! With God's help, love and protection and your positive outlooks, tomorrow promises to get better and better!

I love you both,
Mama

Acknowledgments

I would like to thank all the children, faculty, administration and staff at Merriwether Elementary School who are daily inspirations and reminders that the future can be positive and filled with good character!

Table of Contents

Introduction i

Foreword v

Character ....Days 1-10

Choices ....Days 11-25

Responsibility ....Days 26-39

Kindness ....Days 40-56

Manner ....Days 57-67

Honesty/Integrity ....Days 68-82

Trust ....Days 83-95

Respect ....Days 96-109

Courage ....Days 110-125

Equality..Days 126-133

Sharing/Cooperation ....Days 134-146

Goal Setting ....Days 147-158

Dependability...Days 159-170
Attitude ....Days 171-180
About the Author

Introduction

This book is intended for teachers or school counselors (K-12) to use. The daily character thoughts offered are appropriate for any classroom or school setting (i.e. regular, special education, alternative school, etc.). Ideally, adoption of this program throughout an entire school (or school system) would result in better character habits being practiced -- thus, less discipline problems and less school drop-outs. Repetition and daily reinforcements are key elements when teaching students the life long importance of practicing good character traits. When used, as the author intended, one page in this book may be introduced each morning as a positive way for students and teachers to begin their school day. The exercises can be coupled with Reading, Language Arts and Social Studies lessons.

Character Education is the foundation for all academic, interpersonal relationships, personal and social growth. When good character traits become life long habits for students, more success is possible at home, school and later in the workplace. While character must be stressed in the home, schools have the second greatest influence given the many hours and 180 days of each year children attend.

Who can argue with good character virtues being stressed, such as *Responsibility, Kindness, Good Manners, Honesty/Integrity, Trust, Respect, Courage, Equality, Sharing/Cooperation, Goal Setting, Dependability* and *Positive Attitudes?* These virtues clearly promote better self-esteem, better self-discipline and more positive social interactions.

Following are some specific ideas for the use of this book:

- Morning announcements made by the Principal;

- Discussions held between students with the Teacher as the facilitatior;

- A "Character Line" could be posted at the front of the class (using sentence strips), with daily thoughts added each morning;

- Games (such as "Memory" or "Character Match-ups");

- Student journals reflecting on the good character trait of the day (or several from the previous week) -- It would be great to send these journals home at the end of the year for students to keep!;

- Literature reviews of either autobiographies or biographies of historical figures who modeled great character;

- Small group interventions facilitated by the School Counselor;

- Original poems formulated by cooperative learning groups within the classroom and displayed in the school hallway;

- District wide implementation of the program which could result in school competitions with decreased discipline problems;

- School wide implementation of the program with classroom poster or hall display competitions;

- Classroom implementation with positive reinforcement given children exhibiting good character traits;

- Cooperative small groups within classrooms to formulate additional good character statements;

- Parent/school newsletters publishing student works in regard to the character thoughts;

- Original class dramas which role play good character traits as opposed to less desirable traits (could be done in cooperative groups and performed for the class); and,

- Many, more...!

Each of the thoughts contained in this book is intended to be encouraging and positive. The promotion of a better environment within the classroom, school and/or district is the intended result after a complete year of total implementation. As a reminder throughout the book, *"Good character traits are the results of good choices and must become <u>habits</u>,"*. Only by promoting, repeating and continually modeling can we, as educators, truly make a difference in the lives of our students!

Foreword

I highly recommend Donna Forrest's book, *180 Days of Character*.

Donna is right on the mark with *180 Days of Character*! The key to turning around our families, our schools, our kids, and our Country, is the implementation of Character Education in our public schools through the use of the moral cardinal virtues that have been approved by all of the major religions.

This is why I am so positive for Donna's great work in helping to teach and role-model right over wrong for our current young people who will soon be leading our Nation.

Harry S. Dent*

*Former advisor to Presidents Nixon, Bush & Ford, Billy Graham and Senator Strom Thurmond. Currently involved in Laity Ministries and author of five books, including a primer on Character Education.

Character

Your character is who you really are *inside yourself.*

~ You control the kind of person you want to be - no one else.

~ Practicing good character allows greater peace in your heart.

~ Only you know what you expect of yourself and your actions.

Good character traits can become good life habits!

- Habits are things we repeat over and over.

- If you practice good character traits (such as honesty, respect, responsibility, courage, kindness, etc.) then these traits become life habits.

- Good character habits help us with negative peer pressure (you can say "no" faster since your good character has become a habit).

Good life habits can lead toward a better life!

~ A better life is a more peaceful life.

~ If we practice good life habits, we are more confident in making right choices.

~ Good life habits lead us to friends with similar good life habits.

Your good character can never be taken away from you by anyone but *you!*

~ No one can give you good character OR take good character away from you.

~ If you exercise and practice good character, your good character becomes stronger (just like your muscles become stronger when you exercise them).

~ _____ (your name) is in charge of _____'s good character.

Character involves the way you deal with yourself and others-- both on the outside and the inside.

~ Good character involves self-control - even when you might be angry.

~ Good character carries the responsibility of respecting and being kind to both others and yourself.

~ Good character involves honesty (or integrity) and courage so you can be trusted.

Day 5

Good character equals more life success.

~ Good success is available to anyone who is responsible, dependable, honest, courageous and holds their good character as an important part of their life.

~ Good character can never be taken away from you by anyone other than yourself.

~ You will gain more success by being honest, because others will trust you more.

*Good character helps maintain
integrity through both
good and bad times.*

~ When your life seems in order, you can help others see the
importance of good character.

~ When life is tough you can rely on the good character traits
you have practiced in making hard decisions.

~ If someone chooses to tell things about you that are not
true, your good character will be noticed by others and the
person choosing to gossip will look foolish.

Good character is supported by a positive attitude.

~ Positive attitude means concentrating on good things now and in the future!

~ Think good thoughts!

~ Count your blessings.

Appear positive, think positive, act positive and the character of those around you will improve!

~ Smile and encourage others daily!

~ Think and repeat *only good* thoughts.

~ Let your actions show kindness, good manners and respect toward the ideas of others so others may want to do the same.

Gain peace inside yourself by practicing good character traits such as honesty, respect, responsibility and courage.

∼ When you are honest, you never have to feel guilty.

∼ When you respect others and act responsibly you gain higher self-esteem.

∼ It takes courage to practice good character traits when those around you choose not to do the same, but it's peaceful to know you have chosen the right thing!

Choices

Your character is your choice.

∼ Your parents can teach you good character traits, but *only you* can choose to *live* with good character.

∼ Your teacher or counselor can point out good character traits and the results that follow, but *only you* can choose to *practice* these good character traits.

∼ Your friends can choose the character *they want*, but *only you* answer for the choices *YOU* make.

Your good character is something that can never be taken away from you unless you make the choice to change it.

~ If you are known by others to be honest, that will never change until you tell a lie.

~ If you have good manners and are kind to others, that will remain a part of your character unless you choose to be rude or mean.

~ If you are known to cooperate and care, that will never change until you choose to be selfish.

Day 12

Good choices are available to everyone.

- All people have equal choices to practice and live with good character.

- All people have equal choices to be cooperative and dependable.

- Everyone can make the choice to tell the truth.

We need to make good choices BEFORE we ACT.

~ Think first before making a difficult choice.

~ Sometimes we need to ask someone we trust for advice before we take action.

~ To make a good choice we sometimes need to gather information first before a final decision is made.

Your attitude is your choice.

~ You can choose to obey rules and understand they are made in the best interest of all.

~ You can choose to cooperate and share with a smile.

~ You can choose to think good thoughts and discard bad ones.

Remember -
the SUCCESSFUL ATTITUDE is the
POSITIVE ATTITUDE.

~⌐ You know you can do some things well. Concentrate and practice those things.

~⌐ Set a short-term goal and believe you can reach it by working hard.

~⌐ Look at your blessings such as (your friends, teacher(s), counselor(s), parent(s), family, etc.) go to them for encouragement to keep a positive attitude.

Make a choice to DO YOUR BEST.

～ Practice, practice, practice…at anything you wish to accomplish.

～ Be neat.

～ Try, try, try…persevere and don't give up easily.

Day 17

If you hear someone else talking bad about someone else, make a choice *not* to listen (just walk away).

~~ Walk away, find another person and encourage them.

~~ Say something positive about another person.

~~ Find one good thing about a lonely person and point it out to them.

Make a choice to stay away from those who use bad language.

∼ Bad language never helps anyone feel better about themselves -- including you.

∼ Good character traits only include good, positive statements.

∼ A kind person never needs bad language.

Choose to stay away from all drugs!

~ Alcohol distorts or changes the way you think and actually kills certain brain cells.

~ Smoking cigarettes damages lungs.

~ Marijuana, cocaine and other illegal drugs can destroy your good reputation and character.

Make a choice to develop good posture habits.

~e~ Standing straight and tall shows your self confidence.

~e~ Sitting with good posture is the mannerly way.

~e~ Good posture is healthy for your spine, breathing system, etc.

Proper exercise improves health and character stamina.

~e~ Proper exercise is good for the mind and body.

~e~ Exercise reduces the risk of heart and lung problems.

~e~ When exercising daily, more physical and emotional strength is a result!

Choose to set goals --
both short and long term.

~ An example of a short term goal could be to decide to make better grades or exercise more.

~ An example of a long term goal could be to graduate from high school.

~ A life time goal could be to live and keep good character and a good reputation.

Make a choice to enjoy and improve at least one of your hobbies.

~ If you participate in basketball (or any sport), *practice more.*

~ If you play the piano (or any instrument), *practice more.*

~ If you enjoy working with your hands (building, sewing, etc.), find an adult to help you learn and do more.

Good character is found in good literature -- make a choice to READ more.

~ Read different kinds of factual, but interesting books (for example, autobiographies, biographies, true accounts of historical events, etc.)

~ Investigate the daily newspaper and *look* for "good news".

~ Go to a library on a regular basis.

Responsibility

Responsibility is accepting the results of your own actions.

~ If you have acted unkind to someone, then it is your responsibility to apologize.

~ If you have chosen to tell a lie, then you must be responsible enough to understand why others may not trust you.

~ Sometimes discipline is necessary (for example, if you have misbehaved or broken a class rule).

You are only responsible for yourself.

~ You *cannot* control the actions of *others.*

~ You can only complete *your* responsibilities (for example, your school work, your chores, etc.).

~ Responsibility for yourself includes cleanliness and taking care of your own body.

Decide for your actions to be positive ones.

~ Only share positive or encouraging statements with others.

~ Act in a way that *lifts up* both others and you.

~ Let your face radiate kindness and a positive attitude
   (smile a lot)!

The responsible person does his or her best on any task (even homework)!

~~ The responsible person completes the *whole* job, not just part of it.

~~ Your *best* is the most you can expect of yourself.

~~ Once a task has been started, you must be responsible enough to finish it (even if you don't want to)!

Be responsible in school by following school rules.

∼ School rules are made to protect both you and everyone in the school.

∼ As a part of your school, it is your responsibility to help make it a better place by obeying the rules.

∼ Following school rules models to others your good character traits.

The responsible person is sensitive of other peoples' feelings.

- ~ The responsible person realizes that others who are physically challenged need friends and encouragement.

- ~ The responsible person recognizes those who seem alone and can offer them a helping hand and emotional support.

- ~ The responsible friend knows when a friend is having a hard day and can offer a listening ear.

If there is a bully in the crowd, be responsible by either walking away or letting an adult know immediately.

∼ Your responsible action, where a bully is concerned, may keep someone from being hurt.

∼ When you see someone being bullied by another student, tell an adult immediately so the bully can be stopped.

∼ Quietly walking away from a bully shows your own courage.

Be responsible by staying away from drugs.

~ Drugs can ruin your reputation (good character).

~ Drugs can alter or change the way you think and act.

~ Be responsible by staying away from those who *have* drugs.

Show your responsible character by doing your chores without being reminded.

- ∼ If it is your responsibility to feed your pet each day, do so without being reminded.

- ∼ If your chore is to take out the trash each evening, be responsible by planning a time to do this.

- ∼ When you have several chores to do each week, write out a daily *Responsibility Chart* and post it in your room as a reminder.

Follow school and home rules quietly and responsibly.

~ Never whine!

~ By following rules quietly and responsibly, these rules become life habits.

~ Accept and be thankful for rules made for your protection

If you have a pet, be responsible for feeding and giving it water daily.

~ Healthy pets need food and water just like you do!

~ It takes you being responsible to keep your pet healthy.

~ Pets are not able to fix their own plates, so they need you to be responsible enough to help them each day.

Be responsible by planning ahead.

~⌒ Pack your book bag each night before you go to bed.

~⌒ Choose the clothes you plan to wear the next day before you go to bed (it saves much morning chaos).

~⌒ When you have a school project due in two weeks, make a calendar that tells what needs to be done each day.

When you show a responsible attitude, most adults will trust you to do more on your own.

∼ If you have been responsible by telling the truth, your parents may trust you to go more places.

∼ When you are responsible by having good manners and a kind attitude, other adults notice and are more willing to listen to you when you have a point to be made.

∼ If you show a responsible attitude, adults and friends see you as being more mature than some others your same age.

Be responsible with your money.

~ Save for an emergency.

~ Think before you spend -- "*Do I really need this?*"

~ Have one specific place to keep your money (never leave it in your pockets or laying around).

Kindness

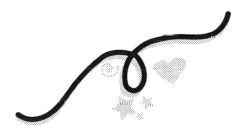

Be Kind to yourself.

~ You are a *priceless* individual!

~ You are special.

~ You have some talents that others do not possess.

Be kind to others.

- ~e Every person is unique and different.

- ~e Every person is special and has worth.

- ~e Every person has *feelings!*

Remember - being kind at *all* times to *all* people never hurts.

~ One day that person you were kind to may be the person who is kind to you when you are having a bad day.

~ Some people have feelings that are more easily hurt than others and they need a kind gesture more often.

~ You may be kind to someone who later becomes famous -- you never know!

Being kind includes choosing for only nice words to leave your mouth.

~~ Choose kind words (for example, *good job, nice smile, etc.*).

~~ Choose to praise others for their good efforts (for example, *way to go, keep up the good work, that's better, etc.*).

~~ Choose to speak with good manners (for example, *please, thank you, excuse me, etc.*).

Be kind to those around you having a "sad day."

~ Offer them a smile and a light pat on the shoulder.

~ Listen if they should want to talk (you do not have to talk as much).

~ Give them some of your time and attention.

Be kind and polite - even when everyone around you seems to be in a hurry.

~ It takes no extra time to smile and be polite.

~ Slow down and help an elderly person who seems to be forgotten in the rush (the grocery store is a good place to help).

~ There is no time limit on kindness.

Sometimes the kindest action is a silent action.

- When someone chooses to gossip, be quiet and do not respond.

- When disagreeing with someone's opinion, sometimes silence is better than engaging in an argument.

- Silence, with a kind facial expression, can be a great action of help to those suffering.

Small acts of kindness are important!

~ Stop and pick up a pencil or book for someone who dropped it.

~ Whisper a word of encouragement to someone feeling sad.

~ Draw a picture or write a kind note to someone who needs an act of kindness today.

K-I-N-D = Kindness Insures that Nice Deeds are done!

~ No matter where you are, if *you* are being kind, then it's a better place!

~ Nice deeds can be insured if you have chosen kindness as one of your good character traits.

~ You can insure comfort and reassure kindness to those around you.

Kind thoughts lead to kind actions.

~ When only kind thoughts are in your mind, only kind actions will result.

~ Kind thoughts are peaceful thoughts.

~ Decide to replace any unkind thought with at least two kind thoughts.

Kind actions cause kind reactions!

∼∾ When you act kind to another person, more than likely they will react kind toward you.

∼∾ If you offer to help someone, usually they react with appreciation and kindness.

∼∾ A sincere, kind, listening attitude will usually result in kindness and thankfulness toward you.

A smile (or a kind expression on our face) - even during the worst of times -- encourages others!

~~ When someone is having a bad day, a simple smile can encourage them.

~~ When someone is angry -- *listen* -- with a sincere look of compassion and a kind facial expression (it will add calmness to the situation).

~~ If a friend has made a bad grade, your kindness and understanding at his or her disappointment will result in them seeing your kind character.

When you are kind to others, you feel better about *yourself.*

∼ If you are kind to others, you have nothing to be ashamed of inside yourself.

∼ When you are kind, but others are not, you can have confidence that you tried your best.

∼ Inner kindness and joy go hand-in-hand and come through in your actions.

The kindness in your heart helps make peacefulness in your mind.

~ Kindness leads us toward peacefulness.

~ The feelings in our heart affect the thoughts in our mind.

~ If your heart is filled with kindness, your mind will be filled with peacefulness.

A kind face shows natural beauty.

~ A smile covers many facial flaws.

~ Kindness is revealed in our eyes.

~ A kind face needs very little make-up!

Always show kindness towards senior citizens or older people.

~e~ Sometimes a senior citizen might need the car door opened.

~e~ In the grocery store a senior citizen may need help unloading his or her cart at the check out counter.

~e~ Take a few minutes to speak to a senior citizen or lonely person this week.

Kind deeds SHOULD be returned.

~ *Always* repay kindness with *more* kindness.

~ Respond to a kindness shown to you by saying, "*Thank you*" or writing a note of thanks.

~ Remember -- parents, teachers and friends all enjoy you returning their kind deeds.

Manners

Good manners exhibit good character choices.

- ～ Good manners are a choice for every one of us!

- ～ When you use good manners, such traits as responsibility, kindness and respect really shine!

- ～ Good character choices may be overlooked by others if you choose poor manners.

Use good manners at school - in the halls, lunchroom and school grounds, as well as the classroom.

- ～ No matter how hurried we are in the halls, the use of good manners is especially needed for safety.

- ～ In the lunchroom at school, good manners help us digest our food better.

- ～ If everyone used good manners on the school ground, there wouldn't be as much pushing, shoving and accidents.

Use good manners at home.

~ Use good manners at the dinner table.

~ Cooperate and share with other family members.

~ Thank other family members when they help you out.

If someone else has bad manners at your table, ignore them. If that doesn't work, ask them to "Please stop."

~ Make conversation with someone else.

~ If someone near you is acting out look the other way.

~ Model good manners for others to see.

Always choose to speak in polite ways.

~ Say "*Hello*" when someone greets you or "*Nice to have seen you*" when leaving.

~ "*Thank you*" or "*No thank you*" are polite ways of accepting or declining an invitation.

~ "*Please*" is necessary when asking for anything.

When in busy lines always remember to say "EXCUSE ME" if you need to get through to another area.

~ Never push or shove.

~ "Excuse me" lets others know you simply want to pass by and are not breaking in line.

~ Using polite language such as "Excuse me" shows you are choosing good manners.

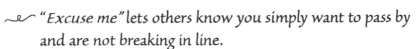

Day 62

Let others finish talking before you begin speaking.

~ Only interrupt if it is an emergency.

~ Listen carefully until the other person finishes talking.

~ Remember -- you can *learn* more by listening to others.

Speak as clearly as possible.

∼ It helps to look at the person to whom you are speaking.

∼ Hold your head up so the person can see you as you speak.

∼ Practice speaking slower, if you tend to run sentences together when you speak too fast.

Speak *calmly* in order to get the best results when you are upset.

~ You cannot look kind and compassionate if you are upset or angry.

~ Crying or screaming makes the message harder to understand.

~ Yelling puts the other person on the defensive and poorer communication results.

When an adult is walking through a door, always stand aside and let the adult go first.

∽ This is an example of showing your respect for others older than you.

∽ By letting an adult go first, your good character and manners are noticed.

∽ When you stand aside for the adult to go first, you are quietly showing that you feel he or she is very important, too.

Remember -- in most public places, it is best to remove your cap or hat when indoors.

∼ Removing your cap or hat is a sign of respect and good manners.

∼ When inside at a school event (such as a play, choral program, etc.) the removal of your cap or hat exhibits respect for those performing.

∼ When attending a patriotic ceremony, the removal of your cap or hat shows respect for our country.

Honesty/Integrity

Being honest shows others your good character.

∼ When others see you as honest, they respect you more as a person.

∼ If you model honesty, there may be others who will follow your lead.

∼ Honest actions yield a good reputation.

Being truthful builds your own self-respect.

~ When you are truthful on the outside, you'll be peaceful on the inside.

~ Respect for yourself can only come with complete truthfulness.

~ You cannot respect yourself if you did not tell the truth.

Being truthful takes courage.

~ Being truthful often means admitting your own mistakes which takes real courage.

~ Being truthful, even when your friends are not, takes real courage.

~ Being truthful when it would benefit you at that moment to cheat, takes true courage.

Cheating equals *Not* being truthful. Remember - cheating eventually hurts you the most in many ways.

~ When you choose to cheat, you have chosen to lie to yourself and others.

~ When you choose to cheat, you are not practicing good character.

~ If someone else sees you cheating, they will lose some of their respect for you.

Being truthful helps keep us safe (remember "The Boy Who Cried Wolf").

~ If you practice always telling the truth, others will believe you.

~ When you constantly tell lies as pranks or jokes, others will not know when you need to be taken seriously.

~ Only dial "911" for an emergency.

Being honest helps others respect you more.

~ Since honesty sometimes requires courage, when you are honest others respect you more.

~ Younger children who admire and respect you may become honest because they watch your example.

~ Teachers and other adults may be reminded of the importance of honesty by watching you and gaining more respect for you.

Honesty is expected.

~ It's against school rules to be dishonest or lie.

~ Parents expect honesty from their children.

~ As you grow and begin to work, your boss expects honesty from you.

Honesty helps others to trust you more.

~ If you are always honest, adults will trust you by allowing you more freedom.

~ If you are always honest, friends will trust you with their concerns because they trust that you'll keep your promises to them.

~ If you are always honest, teachers or employers will trust you as a leader.

Honesty and integrity are parts of real friendships.

- ❧ *Real friendships are special because honesty is a definite part of that relationship.*

- ❧ *Integrity goes together with honesty as a good character trait that must exist in any true friendship.*

- ❧ *No one has a real friendship with a person who tells lies.*

Honesty is for *everyone*.

~ Honesty is for children and adults.

~ Honesty is for rich and poor.

~ Honesty is for short and tall.

Being honest is easy *If* the truth is told the *First* time.

~ A lie can g-r-o-w and cause b-i-g trouble (remember Pinocchio)!

~ One lie can lead to another and another and another until it e-x-p-l-o-d-e-s!

~ If the truth is told the first time, it's easier to go ahead with your life and get past the crisis.

When being honest use good manners -- or tact.

~ If being honest means someone's feelings may be hurt, be kind and explain the full story (not just the hurtful part).

~ Use tact and kindness when being honest.

~ Some things are better left not said (especially if it would hurt the other person's feelings and not accomplish anything good).

You can be trusted when you are honest.

~ When you are honest your family, teachers, counselors and principals trust you.

~ You are trusted because of your ability to be honest and responsible.

~ Honesty builds trust.

Honest actions build good character.

~ℓ Honest actions are responsible actions.

~ℓ Courage and respect are gained by honest actions.

~ℓ Dependability is a good character when strengthened by
   honesty.

Honesty is to friendship as food is to the body.

~ The body cannot grow without food.

~ Real friendship cannot exist without honesty.

~ Honesty in friendship is essential!

Trust

T-R-U-S-T = Trust equals Respect Under Serious Test!

~ Trust must continue no matter what crisis may take place.

~ Trust keeps a respect for the feelings of others regardless of the circumstances.

~ Unless a person is in danger, you must respect their request for keeping a secret.

Trust must be earned by practicing good character traits.

~ Trust comes after honesty is practiced and maintained.

~ Courage to stand for what is right brings about trust.

~ Kindness and respect for others helps trust grow.

Trust is the quiet assurance between family and friends that "all is well" no matter what the circumstances.

~ It's a peaceful, calm feeling of support.

~ It's unconditional love and friendship.

~ Trust is established *before* a crisis.

Trust is believing that what is promised will really happen.

~ Trust is confidence.

~ Trusting that a promise will be fulfilled is believing in that person's good character.

~ Trusting in a person's promise strengthens your relationship with that person.

To break a promise for no good reason destroys trust.

~ A broken promise can shatter dreams.

~ Once the promise is broken it takes a long time to glue the pieces back together.

~ A broken promise (for no good reason) is very similar to a lie.

Trust and faith go together -- hand in hand.

~୧~ Trust has to include faith.

~୧~ It takes faith in a person to trust that person.

~୧~ Both trust and faith in any person are risks.

Be able to trust yourself.

~ Allow yourself honest mistakes.

~ Trust yourself to do the best you can each day.

~ Trust yourself to always strive for good character.

When your thoughts are pure and good, you can trust your actions to be pure and good.

~ Allow only good thoughts to stay in your mind.

~ When bad or mean thoughts keep coming in your mind, talk them over with a parent, teacher or school counselor.

~ Good thoughts will bring kind and good actions.

Be trustworthy and others will trust you to handle more responsibilities.

- Being trustworthy means you already earned the trust and respect of others.

- The more responsible and independent you are the more other people will trust you.

- Both your friends and family will notice your high standards and good character when they realize how trustworthy you really are each day!

Don't let *one honest* mistake
by a friend destroy total trust.

~𝓮 Honest mistakes happen to all of us.

~𝓮 Give a friend or loved one another chance if they make an honest mistake.

~𝓮 Remember that a forgiving heart is needed in all of us -- especially when an honest mistake is made.

Trust history to help you not repeat mistakes.

~ Think about and admit mistakes you have made in the past, so you can try not to make the same mistakes again.

~ If you have been around someone who does not practice good character traits, try to change the "history" of who you choose to hang around with from day to day.

~ If being with a certain friend encourages you to be unkind or disrespectful to others, *don't continue to stay around that person constantly.*

Trust the knowledge and advice of older people who love you.

~ Older people may have had similar life experiences to yours and could save you many heartaches and hurts.

~ Their advice will be in your best interest and for your own good.

~ Sometimes older people who love you can see the "bigger picture" rather than just one event in your life.

Trust is needed everywhere!

~e~ Trust is needed in families and homes.

~e~ Trust is needed in classrooms and schools.

~e~ Trust is needed in friendships.

Respect

Respect yourself.

~ You are special.

~ You deserve the best.

~ Never accept *"put downs"* by others toward you.

Think of one good thing that others respect about you.

~ It may be your overall good character and reputation.

~ It may be your dependability and responsible personality.

~ It may be your ability to smile and bring joy to others.

Respect others by
being courteous and kind.

~✑ Others have worth as human beings.

~✑ Being courteous to others means showing respect and honor toward them as valuable people.

~✑ Kindness is a result of respecting others.

Respect cannot be bought.

~ Respect is priceless -- there is not enough money to buy it!

~ You cannot talk others into respecting you.

~ Respect is a long term benefit of good character habits.

Respect must be earned.

~ Respect, as any good character trait, comes when people see your actions as honest, dependable and courageous.

~ You must work and be responsible in order to earn the respect of others.

~ A positive attitude helps others respect you more.

If we respect authority (or laws), we are much safer.

~ Authority figures (such as parents, principals, teachers, etc.) are here to help keep us safe.

~ Laws are made for our protection.

~ Respect for both authority figures and laws help keep our world safer and more orderly.

Respect the property of others.

~ Be just as careful with another person's property as you are with your own property.

~ Others will be more likely to respect your property when they have watched you show respect for the property of others.

~ By taking care of the property of others there is less room for disagreements.

Respect your body.

~ You only have this one life to take care of your body.

~ A healthy body helps with a healthy mind.

~ Your body is your responsibility.

Respect your physical health by eating properly and exercising regularly.

~℘ Eating properly helps balance the nutrition needed for a healthy body.

~℘ Exercise keeps our heart, lungs and muscles strong and healthy.

~℘ Exercise at least 3-4 times each week (unless a doctor instructs you differently).

Respect your emotional health by allowing yourself some quiet time each day.

~ Quiet time each morning helps you plan and organize your day.

~ When your day seems hurried and hectic, five minutes of quiet time will help you stay calm and more peaceful.

~ When you spend quiet time each evening before going to bed it prepares you for a good night's sleep.

When showing respect for others (parents, teachers friends, etc.), you are setting a good example for those watching you.

~ By respecting your parents, other family members will admire you more.

~ If you show respect for teachers, other classmates will want to do the same.

~ Respect for your friends and their feelings will result in your friends respecting your feelings more.

R-E-S-P-E-C-T = Respect for Excellence Shows People Exceptional Character Traits!

~✐ Doing the best you can do shows others your exceptional character traits.

~✐ Working hard each day in school will show others your exceptional ability to persevere (or continue to try).

~✐ Excellence in character is only achieved by practicing and respecting good character traits at all times.

Day 107

Learn to respect yourself and others by practicing respect daily.

~ Daily, practice respect for your family.

~ Daily, practice respect for those at school.

~ Daily, practice respect for adults you may be in contact with at stores, recreational events, etc.

Respect your teachers.

~ Teachers come to work each day to help you learn so you can be a more successful person.

~ Respect for teachers is necessary practice for the respect needed in any job you may keep in the future.

~ By respecting your teachers, they will respect you!

Courage

It takes courage to ask for help.

~ You must first be aware of the problem and have the courage to find someone who will help.

~ It takes courage to realize you need help.

~ It takes courage to be honest when discussing a problem.

Using your good character even when your friends make wrong choices takes real courage.

~e Courage is choice.

~e Only you make choices for yourself and sometimes it takes courage to make good choices.

~e When friends make poor choices, you must have the courage to stand up for what you believe are better choices.

Remember to go to an adult you can trust (parent, teacher, counselor, principal, etc.) if you have any fears.

~ Sometimes just talking about your fears can make things better!

~ Sometimes an adult or friend is able to get help for you.

~ Many things you fear may never happen. Just talking it over with someone you trust may help you view a more realistic picture.

Learn to admit when you are wrong.
That takes *real* courage!

～ It takes courage to admit you made a mistake rather than try to pass the blame to someone else.

～ When you are wrong, honesty and courage are the good character traits needed immediately to correct the situation.

～ Remember to use courage to admit and face your mistake now, so another *wrong* will not follow!

When setting goals for yourself,
realize courage will be needed
all along the way as you
accomplish those goals.

~ Expect a few *set backs* and be ready with courage to face
them.

~ Keep your thoughts on the goals you have set and continue
to take steps constantly toward those goals.

~ Use courage daily to take the risks or chances needed to
reach your goals.

Realizing your potential and doing your very best in every task takes true courage.

～⌒ Have the courage to examine and use your talents and potential.

～⌒ It takes courage to do your best at all times -- whether in the classroom, on the football field, at the piano, etc.

～⌒ It takes courage to do your best even when you are very tired.

Courage is when you stand for what you know is right.

~ It takes courage to use good character traits when others are not doing the same.

~ It takes courage to say *no* to things that harm your body (alcohol, drugs, etc.)

~ It takes courage to stand up for what you believe is right.

It takes courage to accept those
things you cannot change and
still continue to do the best you
can with what you have now.

~ Sometimes there is no good answer to a problem and it
takes courage to simply accept that.

~ It takes courage to realize you can do your best even when
you could use more help but it's not there.

~ It takes courage to accept friends' choices even when you
know those choices are not good ones.

It takes courage to encourage others.

~~ Encouraging those who have been unkind to you takes real courage.

~~ To encourage those who are less fortunate than you takes special kindness and courage.

~~ To encourage those who are sad takes courage -- sometimes just taking time to listen is all that's needed.

Courage is needed to set goals for yourself and to follow through with determination until your goals are reached.

~~ Perseverance is following through to the end.

~~ Setting goals is a risk and takes real courage.

~~ Determination takes courage.

Courage must be practiced and experienced.

~~ Courage is like our other character traits. It must be practiced to become a habit.

~~ To experience a courageous action or decision results in a positive feeling inside yourself.

~~ Once you realize that your courage has helped others and you, it's easier to have more courage the next time. It's now a part of your personality!

Courage is when you keep the *facts* in your mind -- not gossip or rumors.

~ It takes courage not to listen when others gossip.

~ Sometimes it takes courage to search and find the true facts.

~ It takes courage and wisdom to stay with the main problem and not be led astray by other smaller problems.

It takes courage to accept the things we have no control over.

~ Courage is needed to accept school rules and obey them.

~ It takes courage to accept family rules even when you feel as if these rules are unfair at times.

~ When you cannot change a rule or law, courage and peaceful acceptance is the only answer.

It takes courage to be kind to those who are unkind to you.

~ Courage is needed to be kind to someone that has been mean to you.

~ It takes real courage to be pleasant and kind to someone who seems to be really mad or in a bad mood.

~ Remember your courage and patience with others shows them your strong character.

A loud voice is not a courageous voice.

~ A loud voice may seem demanding, rather than courageous.

~ Courage and strength do not need a loud voice (a firm statement is better).

~ It sometimes takes courage to simply stay calm.

It takes courage to *smile* when you don't really feel like it!

~ When you are under pressure or very tense, it takes courage to smile on the *outside*.

~ A smile can show your good character when others realize you may be sad or mad on the inside.

~ Smiling through tears reminds you and others that better days may be ahead!

Equality

All hearts are the same color.

~ *All people have feelings of happiness, sadness, etc.*

~ *Every person experiences both joys and hurts.*

~ No matter what size, shape, color, or nationality, all people have a heart that needs care.

Person + Person = Persons
(in any combination!)

~ No matter what combination, realize the person next to you has worth.

~ When you are working with another person, find the good points about that person and yourself so you can become a team!

~ You are one-half of a pair of people working together and the other person is equally one-half, so learn to be fair.

When *everyone* works together,
the task is completed faster
and *everyone* is happier.

~ Each person can take a part to complete the whole task.

~ Working together helps new friendships begin.

~ When all people work together, the group becomes stronger.

ALL have worth and potential.

~✐ No one person is of less or more value than another.

~✐ If you practice good character traits you will learn to find
the potential and talents in those around you -- no matter
who you think they may be.

~✐ You cannot put a price tag on any person's worth.

Day 129

Different eyes, hair, skin and personalities make the world a more diverse and attractive place!

∼ The world would be very boring if everyone looked the same!

∼ Our differences make us interesting.

∼ It takes different personalities to handle different tasks.

Self-control can be practiced and learned by ALL, if we just keep trying!

~ A person who becomes angry easily and does not practice self-control, gains a poor reputation.

~ Self-control takes true courage.

~ Self-control can be practiced anytime things don't really go your way.

Even when our circumstances seem unfair, we all are equal in the good we can give to the world.

~ Everyone can contribute something good to the world.

~ When circumstances are unfair, you can show good character by continuing to do the best we can do (and not whining).

~ Never let bitterness follow unfairness. Bitterness only hurts you.

Day 132

Smiles bring positive results!

∼℮‾ Everyone can smile!

∼℮‾ No matter what size, shape, color or nationality, smiles give the same message.

∼℮‾ Positive feelings are causes and results of smiles.

Sharing/Cooperation

Share your friends.

~ Everyone deserves more than one friend.

~ A true friend will appreciate freedom to be around others at times.

~ A friendship can be destroyed if you try to control the other person (for example, who they talk to, go home with, etc.)

Be a good listener.

~ Listening, with an interested ear, must occur in order to share thoughts and ideas.

~ Listening takes time.

~ Friends need and enjoy being heard.

Concentrate on what others tell you
by *looking* at the person as
he or she speaks to you.

～ Looking at a person as you listen, shows your interest in what that person is saying.

～ You can respond better if you have listened well.

～ Listening well helps you understand the other person better.

Day 136

Enjoy sharing!

- Do not be known as selfish! That will hurt your good character!

- If you share, you will give to someone as well as receive from someone.

- Share with a willing heart and it can be more fun!

Sharing is to cooperation as caring is to kindness.

~ Sharing and cooperation are good character traits that go together.

~ Caring and kindness are good character traits that go together.

~ These four things need practice and your willingness to keep up your good character traits.

To cooperate is to work and grow together.

~ It takes more than one person to cooperate.

~ It takes a positive attitude for good cooperation.

~ To cooperate, in most circumstances, takes maturity and good character.

Share and you'll always receive something in return.

~ To share shows a good attitude.

~ Sharing means giving and receiving.

~ When you share with someone, they usually are willing to share with you!

S-H-A-R-E = Share Happiness And Real Experiences.

~e~ Share in good experiences!

~e~ Share in another person's happiness (be happy for them).

~e~ Real experiences are sometimes happy and sometimes sad, so be willing to share with friends either of these experiences.

When sharing ideas with another person and you both decide to keep one idea each – you have successfully made a compromise.

~ Compromises, in any relationship, are sometimes necessary.

~ To cooperate and share, everyone involved must be heard in order to reach a compromise.

~ A successful compromise is a great solution between family and friends.

We must learn to share first and next we must learn to cooperate.

~ When you were 2 or 3 years old you learned to share your toys.

~ Next, in preschool or kindergarten you learned to share your time with other children.

~ Now, you must make a choice to learn to cooperate in school and later in work.

Cooperation is a character trait we must possess.

~ Cooperation brings more success at home and in play.

~ Cooperation brings more success at school.

~ All must cooperate when working together on a project or task.

Team cooperation makes any job easier for each team member.

~ With team cooperation, there's a better chance of winning.

~ When one or two team members choose not to cooperate, it's almost impossible for the team to be successful.

~ When each member does cooperate, each job is smaller and easier to do!

When the band plays a song, each instrument must help out, just as each of us must cooperate (or work together) with each other.

~ If one instrument does not play, the song sounds different.

~ If you choose not to cooperate, the others have a more difficult task.

~ By working together or cooperating, we can make beautiful music!

Goal Setting

Decide to *IMPROVE* on *ONE* thing *TODAY.*

~ Decide to improve on one good character trait that needs more practice.

~ Decide to be more willing to help others.

~ Decide to study harder and listen better in school.

To reach your goal you must persevere.

~ You must keep on trying!

~ You must think positive!

~ You must remember the goal you are working to accomplish.

The word *QUIT* must *NEVER* be in your vocabulary.

~ Replace the word "quit" with the words "keep trying"!

~ Remember - courage is needed to try again and again.

~ Think positive thoughts and the word "quit" won't sneak into your mind as often.

Set daily goals…and keep trying (persevere).

~e~ Each morning set a goal for that day.

~e~ Remind yourself of that goal at lunch.

~e~ Reflect on your success at night.

Set monthly goals...and keep trying (persevere).

~ Decide what needs to be done each week to accomplish that goal successfully.

~ Have a monthly calendar posted in your room.

~ Write the monthly goal across the top.

Set yearly goals…and keep trying (persevere).

~ Decide on one or two major goals to be accomplished during the next year.

~ Write the goal(s) and post in your room.

~ Begin doing the small things needed to reach this bigger, longer term goal.

Little goals accomplished =
Bigger goals mastered.

~ Baby steps led you to begin walking.

~ Small goals met lead to bigger, more successful goals reached.

~ Begin doing the small things needed to reach this bigger, longer term goal.

It takes climbing one step at a time to reach the top of the stairs.

~ When you first learned to climb up the stairs, you crawled a little each time (like you must do when setting a new goal).

~ Then you took one step at a time.

~ Finally, you were able to leap across several steps (it's the same principle as you practice to reach your goal)!

If you fall back one step, decide to climb forward two steps.

~ When you fall down, pick yourself up and try again.

~ Sometimes it takes double effort and more courage to try again and again.

~ Remember -- "quit" is not a word for you. Instead remember to "keep trying" or "persevere".

Talk with someone you trust about your goals.

~ A parent or a family member will help you.

~ Teachers may be able to offer ideas that will help you reach your goals.

~ The school counselor will listen and help you investigate the ways you may reach your goals successfully.

We are sometimes like little puppies. We must run after the ball many times before we become good at bringing it back.

~ You must learn many things before a new goal is reached.

~ You must be willing to chase your dream.

~ Decide to carry your tasks successfully until your goal is accomplished!

Practice…practice…practice helps us be successful!

~ This is one reason for homework!

~ Practice helps you become better at a job.

~ Practice helps you meet your goals.

Dependability

Take the word *CAN'T* out of your vocabulary. Replace it with the word *TRY.*

∼ If you try, you have the courage of taking a risk.

∼ The word *can't* stops you from reaching your dream.

∼ To try gives you a sense of doing your best.

Be enthusiastic and "up beat" about your duties.

~∼ Be excited about your opportunities.

~∼ Your "up beat" or positive attitude makes your duties more enjoyable.

~∼ Enthusiasm is contagious. Be sure to spread it around!

When you make a mistake, simply admit it.

~ Try to learn a better way to handle the problem if it should happen again.

~ Be completely honest and show your courageous character.

~ Everyone makes mistakes, so don't be too hard on yourself.

Decide to be dependable.

~ To be dependable, means you keep your word or promises.

~ Dependability and responsibility are good character traits that others recognize and appreciate.

~ When you are dependable, others trust you more.

When you are dependable, you receive more freedom and responsibilities.

~ With more freedom, you can make more decisions for yourself.

~ As a dependable person, you become more confident as a leader.

~ With more freedom and responsibilities, you become more confident and your self-esteem will improve.

Being dependable means knowing
you will do *what* you are asked
when you are asked to complete it.

~✍ Jobs or tasks you have been assigned will get done on time!

~✍ If an emergency should arise before the task is completed, as a dependable person you should contact someone to let them know of the emergency.

~✍ Being dependable means you will get the job done *right!*

Being able to depend on yourself and your character, helps you build more confidence.

~e With more confidence in yourself, your ability to become a leader increases.

~e When you are able to depend on yourself and your character, less doubts cloud your mind.

~e More confidence means more inner peace.

If you are a part of a team, you *must* be dependable, or the whole team will suffer.

~⌇ Your part of that team is necessary for the team to experience success.

~⌇ It takes little parts together to make a whole.

~⌇ No matter how big or small your part is, the team needs you to complete the whole and they must be able to depend on you!

Being a *true* friend requires dependability.

~ A true friend is one you can count on at all times.

~ Dependability as a friend is the same as honesty is to trusting.

~ Friendships are relationships and *must* include dependability.

Dependability, trustworthiness and honesty are like links in a chain.

～ Dependability, trustworthiness and honesty fit together.

～ These are good character traits that cannot be left out of any good relationship (friendship, family or school).

～ These are three good character traits that must become life habits if you wish for success.

Find one dependable friend and you have the most valuable gift of your life.

∼ This may be a friend you seldom see or talk with, but you know you can depend on them if you have a need.

∼ You can depend on this friend to encourage you when you are down.

∼ You can depend on this friend to be honest with you, even if it hurts a little, because it will help you in the long term.

Day 169

You can receive so much encouragement from a dependable friend.

~ This encouragement could come from a friend near your age.

~ This could be a dependable friend such as a family member.

~ This could be a dependable friend such as your teacher or school counselor.

Attitude

A positive attitude covers many disappointments.

~℮ A positive attitude focuses on the good things ahead.

~℮ A positive attitude realizes there will be some "bumps" to fall over on the path to success.

~℮ A positive attitude keeps trying and moving forward.

Plan to have the most positive attitude *possible*, no matter what the circumstances.

~ This makes your strong, courageous character real to those around you.

~ This positive attitude shows your dependability.

~ Kindness and good choices are seen in people with positive attitudes.

Day 172

Good body posture radiates a good attitude to those around you.

~ Practice sitting, standing and walking with good posture.

~ Good posture radiates to others good self-confidence.

~ If you have good posture, usually a good attitude seems to follow.

A great attitude is like a taste of your favorite candy -- it leaves a delicious taste in your mind and body!

~ You can't feel too bad if your attitude is great!

~ With a great attitude, you feel more positive inside yourself.

~ When you feel positive, the "down times" seem less major.

When a friend is having a bad day,
your positive attitude about your
friendship will encourage them.

~ Your friend will realize you are there for support.

~ Your encouragement to your friend will allow them to have
a more positive attitude.

~ Your positive attitude will support your true friendship.

Walk into your classroom each day with a positive attitude.

~ Think and believe for success in your classwork.

~ Think and believe for success in your relationship with classmates.

~ Think and believe for success with your teachers.

Doing your very best is the most you can expect from yourself.

~ When you have done your best, go to the next task with confidence.

~ When you have done your best, don't look back and wish for more -- be happy with the success you have accomplished!

~ Realize that doing your best does not mean you have to be perfect (no one is perfect)!

Keep an attitude of *patience* with others and yourself.

∼ If you don't solve a problem the first time, have patience to try again.

∼ When not reaching your goal for the day or week, have the patience to think through the difficulty and decide where to go from there.

∼ Everyone requires patience -- both you and others!

Better attitudes lead to better self-control.

~ With a good attitude, you won't loose your temper as often.

~ You can control the words that leave your mouth better if your attitude is positive.

~ Self-control must be practiced just as any of our good character traits. Self-control must become a habit!

A forgiving attitude is a peaceful attitude.

∼ If you have a forgiving attitude you are not keeping bitterness inside you.

∼ If others see your forgiving attitude, their respect for you will grow.

Forgiveness is necessary for a peaceful attitude inside yourself.

About the Author...

Donna Forrest is an Elementary School Counselor and owner/coordinator of Palmetto West Counseling Services. She has earned a Bachelor of Arts degree in Elementary Education and a Master degree and Educational Specialist degree from the University of South Carolina in Counselor Education. Donna is a National Certified Counselor and a Licensed Associate Counselor with the state of South Carolina.

From 1996-97 Donna served as editor of the South Carolina Counseling Association (SCCA) newsletter, *The Palmetto Counselor*. In 1997 she was elected Treasurer-Elect of that organization in which she currently serves as Treasurer. In the South Carolina School Counseling Association (SCSCA), she is Ethics Chair and serves on the

Governing Board for the state. In addition, Donna is a charter member of the American Association of Christian Counselors (AACC) and American Counseling Association (ACA).

Donna is the organist for First Baptist Church of Belvedere, South Carolina, where she also teaches a high school Sunday School class. She lives in North Augusta, South Carolina with her two children, Derek (age 17) and April (age 14) and their dog Abby.